P9-ELV-917

To

_____

From

_____

Date

_____

FAMILY
CHRISTIAN
PRESS

Just for Kids

31 Daily Devotions

Self-Esteem

Copyright ©2006 Family Christian Press

All rights reserved. No part of this book may be reproduced, stored in a retrieval system, or transmitted in any form or by any means—electronic, mechanical, photocopying, recording, or any other—except for brief quotations in printed reviews, without prior written permission of the publisher.

FAMILY CHRISTIAN PRESS
Grand Rapids, MI 49530

The quoted ideas expressed in this book (but not scripture verses) are not, in all cases, exact quotations, as some have been edited for clarity and brevity. In all cases, the author has attempted to maintain the speaker's original intent. In some cases, quoted material for this book was obtained from secondary sources, primarily print media. While every effort was made to ensure the accuracy of these sources, the accuracy cannot be guaranteed. For additions, deletions, corrections or clarifications in future editions of this text, please write FAMILY CHRISTIAN PRESS.

Scripture quotations are taken from:

The Holy Bible, King James Version

The Holy Bible, New International Version (NIV) Copyright © 1973, 1978, 1984, by International Bible Society. Used by permission of Zondervan Publishing House. All rights reserved.

The Holy Bible, New King James Version (NKJV) Copyright © 1982 by Thomas Nelson, Inc. Used by permission.

The New American Standard Bible®, (NASB) Copyright © 1960, 1962, 1963, 1968, 1971, 1972, 1973, 1975, 1977, 1995 by The Lockman Foundation. Used by permission.

Holy Bible, New Living Translation, (NLT)copyright © 1996. Used by permission of Tyndale House Publishers, Inc., Wheaton, Illinois 60189. All rights reserved.

The Message (MSG)- This edition issued by contractual arrangement with NavPress, a division of The Navigators, U.S.A. Originally published by NavPress in English as THE MESSAGE: The Bible in Contemporary Language copyright 2002-2003 by Eugene Peterson. All rights reserved.

New Century Version®. (NCV) Copyright © 1987, 1988, 1991 by Word Publishing, a division of Thomas Nelson, Inc. All rights reserved. Used by permission.

The Holman Christian Standard Bible™ (HCSB) Copyright © 1999, 2000, 2001 by Holman Bible Publishers. Used by permission.

International Children's Bible®, New Century Version®. (ICB) Copyright © 1986, 1988, 1999 by Tommy Nelson™, a division of Thomas Nelson, Inc. All rights reserved. Used by permission.

Cover Design and Page Layout by Bart Dawson

ISBN 1-58334-360-1

Printed in the United States of America

Just for Kids

Self-Esteem

Table of Contents

A Message for Parents

If your child's bookshelf is already spilling over with a happy assortment of good books for kids, congratulations—that means you're a thoughtful parent who understands the importance of reading to your child.

This little book is an important addition to your child's library. It is intended to be read by Christian parents to their young children. The text contains 31 brief chapters, one for each day of the month. Each chapter consists of a Bible verse, a brief story or lesson, kid-friendly quotations from notable Christian thinkers, a tip, and a prayer. Every chapter examines a different aspect of an important topic: self-esteem.

For the next 31 days, take the time to read one chapter each night to your child, and then spend a few moments talking about the chapter's meaning. By the end of the month, you will have had 31 different opportunities to share God's wisdom with your son or daughter, and that's good . . . very good.

If you have been touched by God's love and His grace, then you know the joy that He has brought into your own life. Now it's your turn to share His message with the boy or girl whom He has entrusted to your care. Happy reading! And may God richly bless you and your family now and forever.

Jesus Loves You

I've loved you the way
my Father has loved me.
Make yourselves at home in my love.
The Words of Jesus (John 15:9 MSG)

ave you heard the song "Jesus Loves Me?" Probably so. It's a happy song that should remind you of this important fact: Jesus loves you very much.

When you invite Jesus into your heart, He will be your friend forever. If you make mistakes, He'll still be your friend. When you aren't perfect, He'll still love you. If you feel sorry or sad, He can help you feel better.

Yes, Jesus loves you . . . and you should love yourself. So the next time you feel sad about yourself . . . or something that you've done . . . remember that Jesus loves you, your family loves you, and you should feel that way, too.

Jesus loves me! This I know, for the Bible
tells me so. Little ones to him belong;
they are weak, but he is strong.
Yes, Jesus loves me! Yes, Jesus loves me!
Yes, Jesus loves me! The Bible tells me so.

Anna B. Warner and Susan Warner

Live your lives in love, the same sort of love
which Christ gives us, and which He
perfectly expressed when He gave Himself
as a sacrifice to God.

Corrie ten Boom

Tip of the Day

There's Only One You! Nobody else in the
world is exactly like you. When God made you,
He made a very special, one-of-a-kind person.
So don't forget this fact: you're very, very,
very, very, very special.

Prayer of the Day

Dear Lord, Jesus loves me.
Let me share His love with
others so that through me,
they can understand
what it means to follow Him.
Amen

God Loves You

We love Him because He first loved us.
1 John 4:19 NKJV

Does God love you? Of course He does! In fact, God loves you so much that He sent His Son Jesus to come to this earth . . . for you! When you accept Jesus into your heart, God gives you a gift that is more precious than gold: that gift is called "eternal life" which means that you will live forever with God in heaven!

You don't have to be perfect to earn God's love . . . you simply have to accept His love by accepting His Son. So do yourself a favor right now: accept God's love with open arms and welcome His Son Jesus into your heart. When you do, your life will be changed today, tomorrow, and forever.

Love is not something God does;
love is something God is.

Beth Moore

Love, for instance, is not something God has
which may grow or diminish or cease to be.
His love is the way God is, and when
He loves, He is simply being Himself.

A. W. Tozer

Tip of the Day

Remember: God's love for you is too big to understand with your brain . . . but it's not too big to feel with your heart.

Prayer of the Day

Dear Lord, the Bible teaches me that
Your love lasts forever. Thank You,
God, for Your love. Let me trust
Your promises, and let me live
according to Your teachings,
not just for today, but forever.
Amen

Don't Be Too Hard on Yourself

You know the Lord is full of mercy and is kind.

James 5:11 NCV

Face facts: nobody's perfect . . . not even you! And remember this: it's perfectly okay not to be perfect. In fact, God doesn't expect you to be perfect, and you shouldn't expect yourself to be perfect, either.

Are you one of those people who can't stand to make a mistake? Do you think that you must please everybody all the time? When you make a mess of things, do you become terribly upset? If so, here's some advice: DON'T BE SO HARD ON YOURSELF!

Even if you're a very good person, you're bound to make mistakes . . . lots of mistakes. When you make a mistake—or when you feel that you haven't "measured up"—you shouldn't become too upset.

Mistakes happen . . . it's simply a fact of life, and it's simply a part of growing up. So don't be too hard on yourself, especially if you've learned something along the way.

God is not hard to please. He does not
expect us to be absolutely perfect.
He just expects us to keep moving toward
Him and believing in Him, letting Him work
with us to bring us into conformity
to His will and ways.

Joyce Meyer

What makes a Christian a Christian
is not perfection but forgiveness.

Max Lucado

Tip of the Day

It's okay to be less than perfect: you don't
have to be perfect to be wonderful.

Prayer of the Day

Dear Lord, help me be kind
to everybody, including myself.
And when I make a mistake,
help me to forgive myself, just like
I forgive other people when
they make mistakes.
Amen

When You Feel Sad

You will be sad,
but your sadness will become joy.
John 16:20 NCV

Sometimes, you feel happy, and sometimes you don't. When you're feeling sad, here are two very important things you should do:

1. Talk to your parents about your feelings.
2. Talk to God about your feelings.

Talking with your parents is helpful because your mom and dad understand this: The problems that seem VERY BIG to you today, probably won't seem so big tomorrow.

Talking with God helps because God hears your prayers and He helps make things better.

So the next time you're sad, don't hold your feelings inside—talk things over with your parents and with God. When you do, you'll feel better . . . and so will they!

God is good, and heaven is forever.
These two facts should brighten up
even the darkest day.

Marie T. Freeman

A sad soul can kill you far quicker
than a germ.

John Steinbeck

Tip of the Day

Everybody feels sad from time to time . . .
but the Bible promises in a little while your
sadness will turn to joy.

Prayer of the Day

Dear Lord, when I am sad,
I know that I can talk to my parents . . .
and to You. Thank You, Lord,
for listening to me. And thank You
for parents who love me
and listen to me.
Amen

You're Special

For you made us only a little lower than God,
and you crowned us with glory and honor.

Psalm 8:5 NLT

When God made you, He made you in a very special way. In fact, you're a wonderful, one-of-a-kind creation, a special person unlike any other.

Do you realize how special you are? Do you know that God loves you because of who you are (not because of the things you've done)? And do you know that God has important things for you to do? Well, whether you realize it or not, all these things are true.

So the next time you feel bad about something you've done, take a look in the mirror, and remember that you're looking at a wonderfully special person . . . you!

God loves you; your parents love you; your family loves you . . . and that's the way that you should feel about yourself, too.

It is what a man thinks of himself
that really determines his fate.

Henry David Thoreau

He who is able to love himself
is able to love others also.

Paul Tillich

Tip of the Day

Accept God's love . . . and love God in
return. God loves you for who you are, not
because of the things you've done. So open
your heart to God's love . . . when you do,
you'll feel better about everything, including
yourself.

Prayer of the Day

Dear Lord, You only made one me,
and I know that You love me
very, very much. I thank You for
Your love, Lord, and I thank You
for the gift of Your Son Jesus.
Amen

A Loving Family...
Like Yours!

Show family affection to one another
with brotherly love.
Outdo one another in showing honor.

Romans 12:9–10 HCSB

Your family is a wonderful, one-of-a-kind gift from God. And your family members love you very much—what a blessing it is to be loved!

Have you ever really stopped to think about how much you are loved? Your parents love you (of course) and so does everybody else in your family. But it doesn't stop there. You're also an important part of God's family . . . and He loves you more than you can imagine.

What should you do about all the love that comes your way? You should accept it; you should be thankful for it; and you should share it . . . starting now!

Money can build or buy a house.
Add love to that and you have a home.
Add God to that and you have a temple.
You have "a little colony of
the kingdom of heaven."

Anne Ortlund

Tip of the Day

Since you love your family . . . let them know
it by the things you say and the things you
do. And, never take your family members
for granted; they deserve your very best
treatment!

Prayer of the Day

Dear Lord, You have given me a family
that cares for me and loves me.
Thank You. Let me love everybody
in my family, even when they're not
perfect. And let me always be thankful
that my family loves me even when
I'm not perfect.
Amen

How You Look . . . on the Inside and the Outside

Blessed are the pure in heart,
because they will see God.
Matthew 5:8 HCSB

Other people see you from the outside, and sometimes people will judge you by the way you look. But God doesn't care how you look on the outside. Why? Because God is wiser than that; God cares about what you are on the inside—God sees your heart.

If you're like most people, you'll worry a little bit about the way you look (or maybe you worry a lot about it). But please don't worry too much about your appearance!

How you look on the outside isn't important . . . but how you feel on the inside is important. So don't worry about trying to impress other people. Instead of trying to impress other kids, try to impress God by being the best person you can be.

Snuggle in God's arms. When you are hurting,
when you feel lonely or left out,
let Him cradle you, comfort you, reassure
you of His all-sufficient power and love.

Kay Arthur

I think God knew that the message we
sometimes need to hear today is not what
a great and mighty God we serve,
but rather what a tender, loving Father
we have, even when He says no.

Lisa Whelchel

Tip of the Day

Beauty on the outside isn't important . . .
beauty on the inside is.

Prayer of the Day

Dear Lord, You know my heart.
Help me to say things,
to do things, and to think things
that are pleasing to You.
Amen

When People Aren't Nice

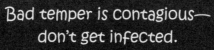

Bad temper is contagious—
don't get infected.

Proverbs 22:25 MSG

Sometimes, young people can be very mean. They can make fun of other people, and when they do, it's wrong. As Christians, we should be kind to everyone. And, if other kids say unkind things to someone, we should never join in.

Today and every day, make sure that you're a person who is known for the kind way that you treat everybody. That's how God wants you to behave.

And if someone says something to you that isn't very nice, don't pay too much attention. Just forgive that person as quickly as you can, and try to move on . . . as quickly as you can.

Never allow anyone to rain on your parade
and thus cast a pall of gloom
and defeat on the entire day.

Og Mandino

No one can make you jealous, angry,
vengeful, or greedy . . . unless you let him.

Napoleon Hill

Tip of the Day

Remember to forgive: If you can't find it in
your heart to forgive those who have hurt
you, you're hurting yourself more than you're
hurting anyone else.

Prayer of the Day

Dear Lord, sometimes it's very hard to forgive those who have hurt me, but with Your help, I can forgive them. Help me to bring forgiveness into my heart, so that I can forgive others just as You have already forgiven me.

Amen

Keep On Trying

Be on guard. Stand true to what you believe.
Be courageous. Be strong.

1 Corinthians 16:13 NLT

When things don't turn out right, it's easy for most of us to give up. But usually, it's wrong. Why are we tempted to give up so quickly? Perhaps it's because we're afraid that we might embarrass ourselves if we tried hard but didn't succeed.

Here's something to remember: if you're having a little trouble getting something done, don't get mad, don't get frustrated, don't get discouraged, and don't give up. Just keep trying . . . and keep believing in yourself.

When you try hard—and keep trying hard— you can do amazing things . . . but if you quit at the first sign of trouble, you'll miss out. So here's a good rule to follow: when you have something that you want to finish, be brave enough (and wise enough) to finish it . . . you'll feel better about yourself when you do.

God never gives up on you,
so don't you ever give up on Him.

Marie T. Freeman

We are all on our way somewhere.
We'll get there if we just keep going.

Barbara Johnson

Tip of the Day

If things don't work out at first, don't quit. If you never try, you'll never know how good you can be.

Prayer of the Day

Dear Lord, sometimes I feel like giving up. When I feel that way, help me do the right thing . . . and help me finish the work You want me to do.

Amen

Doing the Right Thing

The godly walk with integrity;
blessed are their children after them.

Proverbs 20:7 NLT

When you know that you're doing what's right, you'll feel better about yourself. Why? Because you have a little voice in your head called your "conscience." Your conscience is a feeling that tells you whether something is right or wrong—and it's a feeling that makes you feel better about yourself when you know you've done the right thing.

Your conscience is an important tool. Pay attention to it!

The more you listen to your conscience, the easier it is to behave yourself. So here's great advice: first, slow down long enough to figure out the right thing to do—and then do it! When you do, you'll be proud of yourself . . . and other people will be proud of you, too.

A man who lives right, and is right,
has more power in his silence
than another has by his words.

Phillips Brooks

When we do what is right, we have
contentment, peace, and happiness.

Beverly LaHaye

Tip of the Day

When you choose to do the right thing . . .
you make everybody happy. You make your
parents happy; you make your teachers happy;
you make your friends happy; and you make
God happy!

Prayer of the Day

Dear Lord, help me to slow down
and to think about my behavior.
And then, help me to do the right
thing, so that I can feel better about
myself . . . and You can, too.
Amen

When You're Worried

Jesus said,
"Don't let your hearts be troubled.
Trust in God, and trust in me."
John 14:1 NCV

When you're worried, it helps to talk about the things that are troubling you. And who can you talk to? Well for starters, you can talk to your parents and you can talk to God.

If you're worried about something, you can pray about it any time you want. And remember that God is always listening, and He always wants to hear from you.

So when you're worried, try this plan: talk and pray. Talk to the grownups who love you, and pray to the Heavenly Father who made you. The more you talk and the more you pray, the better you'll feel.

Worry is a complete waste of energy.
It solves nothing. And it won't solve that
anxiety on your mind either.

Charles Swindoll

When you are anxious, it means that you
aren't trusting God completely;
it means that you aren't trusting God
to take care of your needs.

Stormie Omartian

Tip of the Day

Worried about something you said or did? If
you made a mistake yesterday, the day to fix it
is today. Then, you won't have to worry about
it tomorrow.

Prayer of the Day

Dear Lord, when I am worried, I know where to turn for help: to those who love me, and to You. Thank You, for the people who love and care for me, and thank You, Lord, for Your love. Because of that love, I have hope and assurance for this day and every day.

Amen

Growing Up Day by Day

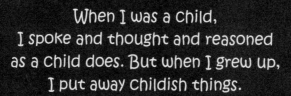

When I was a child,
I spoke and thought and reasoned
as a child does. But when I grew up,
I put away childish things.

1 Corinthians 13:11 NLT

You're growing up day by day, and it's a wonderful thing to watch. Every day, you're learning new things and doing new things. Good for you!

And when should you stop growing up? Hopefully never! That way, you'll always be learning more and doing more.

Do you think it's good to keep growing and growing and growing? If you said "yes," you're right. So remember: you're a very special person today . . . and you'll be just as special when you've grown a little bit more tomorrow.

No matter what we are going through,
no matter how long the waiting for answers,
of one thing we may be sure.
God is faithful. He keeps His promises.
What He starts, He finishes . . . including
His perfect work in us.

Gloria Gaither

Being childlike is commendable.
Being childish is unacceptable.

Charles Swindoll

Tip of the Day

Grown-ups still have plenty to learn . . . and so do you!

Prayer of the Day

Dear Lord, Thank You for letting me
grow a little bit more every day.
I thank You for the person I am . . .
and for the person I can become.
Amen

Friends Who Behave Themselves

As iron sharpens iron,
so people can improve each other.
Proverbs 27:17 NCV

One way that you can feel better about yourself is by staying out of trouble. And one way that you can stay out of trouble is by making friends with people who, like you, want to do what's right.

Are your friends the kind of kids who encourage you to behave yourself? If so, you've chosen your friends wisely. But if your friends try to get you in trouble, perhaps it's time to think long and hard about making some new friends.

Whether you know it or not, you're probably going to behave like your friends behave. So pick out friends who make you want to behave better, not worse. When you do, you'll feel better about yourself . . . a whole lot better.

If you choose to awaken a passion for God,
you will have to choose your friends wisely.

Lisa Bevere

Friends are like a quilt with lots of different
shapes, sizes, colors, and patterns of fabric.
But the end result brings you warmth and
comfort in a support system that
makes your life richer and fuller.

Suzanne Dale Ezell

Tip of the Day

If you choose friends who behave themselves
. . . you'll be far more likely to behave
yourself, too.

Prayer of the Day

Dear Lord, thank You for my friends.
Let me be a good friend to other
people, and let me show them what
it means to be a good Christian.
Amen

Good Thinking

Those who are pure in their thinking are happy, because they will be with God.

Matthew 5:8 NCV

Do you try to think good thoughts about your friends, your family, and yourself? The Bible says that you should. Do you lift your hopes and your prayers to God many times each day? The Bible says that you should. Do you say "no" to people who want you to do bad things or think bad thoughts? The Bible says that you should.

The Bible teaches you to guard your thoughts against things that are hurtful or wrong. So remember this: When you turn away from bad thoughts and turn instead toward God and His Son Jesus, you will be protected . . . and you will be blessed.

If you want to know whether you're thinking correctly, check it out in the Word.

Charles Stanley

People who do not develop and practice good thinking often find themselves at the mercy of their circumstances.

John Maxwell

Tip of the Day

Good thoughts can lead you to some very good places . . . and bad thoughts can lead elsewhere. So guard your thoughts accordingly.

Prayer of the Day

Dear Lord, You teach me that
my thoughts are important to You.
Help me to think good thoughts and
to do good deeds, today and every day.
Amen

God Wants the Best for You

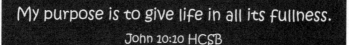

My purpose is to give life in all its fullness.
John 10:10 HCSB

Here are three things to think about:

1. God loves you.

2. God wants what's best for you.

3. God has a plan for you.

God's plan may not always happen exactly like you want, but remember: God always knows best. Sometimes, even though you may want something very badly, you must still be patient and wait for the right time to get it, And the right time, of course, is determined by God.

Even if you don't get exactly what you want today, you can be sure that God wants what's best for you . . . today, tomorrow, and forever.

Jesus intended for us to be overwhelmed by the blessings of regular days. He said it was the reason He had come: "I am come that they might have life, and that they might have it more abundantly."

Gloria Gaither

Jesus wants Life for us, Life with a capital L.

John Eldredge

Tip of the Day

Don't miss out on God's gifts: Every day is a beautifully wrapped gift from God. Unwrap it, and give thanks to the Giver.

Prayer of the Day

Dear Lord, You are my Teacher.
Help me to learn from You. And then,
let me show others what it means to be
a kind, generous, loving Christian.
Amen

You Don't Have to be Perfect

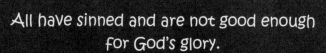

All have sinned and are not good enough for God's glory.
Romans 3:23 NCV

If you're trying to be perfect, you're trying to do something that's impossible. No matter how much you try, you can't be a perfect person . . . and that's okay.

God doesn't expect you to live a mistake-free life—and neither should you. In the game of life, God expects you to try, but He doesn't always expect you to win. Sometimes, you'll make mistakes, but even then, you shouldn't give up!

So remember this: you don't have to be perfect to be a wonderful person. In fact, you don't even need to be "almost-perfect." You simply must try your best and leave the rest up to God.

Excellence is not perfection,
but essentially a desire to be strong in
the Lord and for the Lord.

Cynthia Heald

There was never a person who did
anything worth doing that did not receive
more than he gave.

Henry Ward Beecher

Tip of the Day

If you hear a little voice inside your head
telling you that you'll never be good enough . . .
don't' pay attention to that little voice. God
loves you . . . and if you're good enough for
God, you're good enough.

Prayer of the Day

Dear Lord, help me remember
that I don't have to be perfect
to be wonderful.
Amen

Teamwork Works!

A kingdom that is divided cannot continue,
and a family that is divided cannot continue.

Mark 3:24-25 NCV

Helping other people can be fun! When you help others, you feel better about yourself—and you'll know that God approves of what you're doing.

A kingdom that is divided cannot continue, and a family that is divided cannot continue.

When you learn how to cooperate with your family and friends, you'll soon discover that it's more fun when everybody works together.

So do everybody a favor: learn better ways to share and better ways to cooperate. It's the right thing to do.

Alone we can do so little.
Together we can do so much.
Helen Keller

It is through cooperation,
rather than conflict, that your greatest
successes will be derived . . . .
Ralph Charell

Tip of the Day

Cooperation pays: When you cooperate with your friends and family, you'll feel good about yourself—and your family and friends will feel good about you, too.

Prayer of the Day

Dear Lord, help me learn to be kind,
courteous, and cooperative
with my family and with my friends.
Amen

You Can't Please Everybody

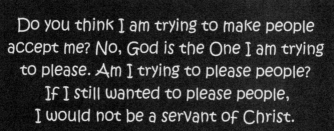

Do you think I am trying to make people accept me? No, God is the One I am trying to please. Am I trying to please people? If I still wanted to please people, I would not be a servant of Christ.

Galatians 1:10 NCV

A re you one of those people who tries to please everybody in sight? If so, you'd better watch out! After all, if you worry too much about pleasing your friends, you may not worry enough about pleasing God.

Whom will you try to please today: your God or your pals? The answer to that question should be simple. Your first job is to obey God's rules . . . and that means obeying your parents, too!

So don't worry too much about pleasing your friends or neighbors. Try, instead, to please your heavenly Father and your parents. No exceptions.

You should forget about trying to be popular with everybody and start trying to be popular with God Almighty.

Sam Jones

Don't be addicted to approval. Follow your heart. Do what you believe God is telling you to do, and stand firm in Him and Him alone.

Joyce Meyer

Tip of the Day

Please God first. Then, work very hard to please your parents.

Prayer of the Day

Dear Lord, help me remember
that I don't have to please everybody
. . . but that I should always
try to please You!
Amen

When You Help Other People, You Feel Better About Yourself

So let us try to do what makes peace and helps one another.

Romans 14:19 NCV

Sometimes, we would like to help make the world a better place, but we're not sure how to do it. Jesus told the story of the "Good Samaritan," a man who helped a fellow traveler when no one else would. We, too, should be good Samaritans when we find people who need our help. A good place to start helping other people is at home. And of course, we should also offer our help at school and at church.

Another way that we can help other people is to pray for them. God always hears our prayers, so we should talk with Him as often as we can. When we do, we're not only doing a wonderful thing for the people we pray for, we're also doing a wonderful thing for ourselves, too. Why? Because we feel better about ourselves when we're helping other people. And the more we help others, the better we should feel about ourselves.

We can't help everyone,
but everyone can help someone.

Loretta Scott

We must not slacken our efforts to do good
to all, especially to those with needs
that will not be met if we fail in our
common task of service to humanity.

Danny Thomas

Tip of the Day

Someone very near you may need a helping
hand or a kind word, so keep your eyes open,
and look for people who need your help,
whether at home, at church, or at school.

Prayer of the Day

Dear Lord, let me help others in every
way that I can. Jesus served others;
I can too. I will serve other people
with my good deeds and with my
prayers. And, I will give thanks for
all those who serve and protect
our nation and our world.

Amen

Loving Everybody
(Including Yourself)

Above all, love each other deeply, because
love covers a multitude of sins.

1 Peter 4:8 NIV

The Bible teaches you this lesson: you should love everybody—and the word "everybody" includes yourself. Do you treat yourself with honor and respect? You should. After all, God created you in a very special way, and He loves you very much. And if God thinks you are amazing and wonderful, shouldn't you think about yourself in the same way? Of course, you should!

So remember this: God wants you to love everybody, including the person you see when you look in the mirror. And one more thing: when you learn how to respect the person in the mirror, you'll be better at respecting other people, too.

You are valuable because God values you.

Stanley Grenz

Being loved by Him whose opinion matters
most gives us the security to risk loving, too—
even loving ourselves.

Gloria Gaither

Tip of the Day

God loves you . . . and you should too.

Prayer of the Day

Dear Lord, Your love is so wonderful
that I can't really imagine it,
but I can share it . . . and I will . . .
today and every day.
Amen

The Person in the Mirror

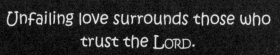

Unfailing love surrounds those who
trust the LORD.
Psalm 32:10 NLT

D o you really like the person you see when you look into the mirror? You should! After all, the person in the mirror is a very special person who is made—and loved—by God.

In fact, you are loved in many, many ways: God loves you, your parents love you, and your family loves you, for starters. So you should love yourself, too.

So here's something to think about: since God thinks you're special, and since so many people think you're special, isn't it about time for you to agree with them? Of course, it is! It's time to say, "You're very wonderful and very special," to the person you see in the mirror.

It is not enough to love ourselves;
we must also like ourselves.

Joyce Meyer

Knowing God's sovereignty and unconditional
love imparts a beauty to life . . . and to you.

Kay Arthur

Tip of the Day

Remember: God loves you, and lots of people
love you, too . . . so it's only proper that
you should admit that you're a very special
person.

Prayer of the Day

Dear Lord, today and every day,
I will do my best to love everybody
. . . including myself.
Amen

DAY 22

Friends Who Are Kind

A friend loves you all the time.
Proverbs 17:17 ICB

Are your friends kind to you? And are your friends nice to other people, too? If so, congratulations! If not, it's probably time to start looking for a few new friends. After all, it's really not very much fun to be around people who aren't nice to everybody.

The Bible teaches that a pure heart is a wonderful blessing. It's up to each of us to fill our hearts with love for God, love for Jesus, and love for all people. When we do, we feel better about ourselves.

Do you want to be the best person you can be? Then invite the love of Christ into your heart and share His love with your family and friends. And remember that lasting love always comes from a pure heart . . . like yours!

Without kindness, there can be no true joy.

Thomas Carlyle

He who sows courtesy reaps friendship,
and he who plants kindness gathers love.

St. Basil

Tip of the Day

Remember the first rule of friendship: it's the Golden one, and it starts like this: "Do unto others . . ." You should practice the Golden Rule, and your friends should practice it, too.

Prayer of the Day

Dear Lord, I thank You for friends
who help me feel better about myself.
Help me to choose my friends wisely,
and help me treat my friends like
I want them to treat me.
Amen

A Rule That's Golden

When you do things, do not let selfishness or pride be your guide. Instead, be humble and give more honor to others than to yourselves.

Philippians 2:3 NCV

Would you like to make the world a better place and feel better about yourself at the same time? If so, you can start by practicing the Golden Rule.

The Bible teaches us to treat other people with respect, kindness, courtesy, and love. When we do, we make other people happy, we make God happy, and we feel better about ourselves, too.

So if you're wondering how to make the world—and your world—a better place, here's a great place to start: let the Golden Rule be your rule. And if you want to know how to treat other people, ask the person you see every time you look into the mirror. The answer you receive will tell you exactly what to do.

Seek to do good, and you will find that
happiness will run after you.

James Freeman Clarke

Make the most of today.
Translate your good intentions into
actual good deeds.

Grenville Kleiser

Tip of the Day

What's good for you is good for them, too.
If you want others to treat you according to
the Golden Rule, then you should be quick to
treat them in the same way. In other words,
always play by the rule: the Golden Rule.

Prayer of the Day

Dear Lord, help me always to do
my very best to treat others as I wish
to be treated. The Golden Rule is
Your rule, Father; let me also
make it mine.

Amen

Too Concerned with Stuff?

Yes, a person is a fool to store up
earthly wealth but not have
a rich relationship with God.

Luke 12:21 NLT

Here's something to remember about stuff: It's not that important!

Lots of people are in love with money and the things that money can buy. God is not. God cares about people, not possessions, and so must you.

You should not be too concerned about the clothes you wear, or the things you own. And above all, don't ever let your self-esteem depend upon the things that you (or your parents) own.

The stuff that you own isn't nearly as important as the love that you feel in your heart—love for your family, love for your friends, and love for your Father in heaven.

We own too many things that aren't
worth owning.

Marie T. Freeman

Poverty is not the absence of goods,
but rather the overabundance of desire.

Plato

Tip of the Day

Stuff Made Simple: The world says, "Buy
more stuff." God says, "Stuff isn't important."
Believe God.

Prayer of the Day

Dear Lord, help me remember that
the stuff I own isn't very important.
What's really important is the love
that I feel in my heart for my family,
the love that I feel for Jesus,
and the love that I feel for You.
Amen

When You Make Mistakes

The Lord says, "Forget what happened
before, and do not think about the past.
Look at the new thing I am going to do.
It is already happening. Don't you see it?
I will make a road in the desert
and rivers in the dry land.

Isaiah 43:18-19 NCV

Are you perfect? Certainly not! No matter how hard you try to do the right thing, you're bound to make mistakes every once in a while . . . everybody does.

When you make a mistake, what should you do about it? Here are two things you should do:

1. Try very hard to learn something from your mistake; that way, you won't make that same mistake again.

2. If you have hurt someone—or if you have disobeyed God—you must ask for forgiveness. That means saying you're sorry to the person you hurt . . . and it also means saying you're sorry to God.

So remember this: if you make a mistake, learn from it. And don't repeat it. Because the biggest mistake you can make is to keep making the same mistake over and over and over again.

The greatest mistake you can make is to be
continually fearing you will make one.

Elbert Hubbard

When you blunder, blunder forward.

Thomas Edison

Tip of the Day

Fix it sooner rather than later: If you make
a mistake, the time to make things better is
now, not later! The sooner you admit your
mistake, the better.

Prayer of the Day

Dear Lord, sometimes I make mistakes.
When I do, forgive me, Father.
And help me learn from my mistakes
so that I can be a better person
and a better example to
my friends and family.
Amen

Saying the Right Thing

Watch the way you talk. Let nothing foul or dirty come out of your mouth. Say only what helps, each word a gift.

Ephesians 4:29 MSG

Your words can help people . . . or not. Make certain that you're the kind of person who says helpful things, not hurtful things. You'll feel better about yourself when you help other people feel better about themselves.

Do you like for people to say kind words to you? Of course you do! And that's exactly how other people feel, too. That's why it's so important to say things that make people feel better, not worse.

Everybody needs to hear kind words, and that's exactly the kind of words they should hear from you!

A lot of people have gone further than they thought they could because someone else thought they could.

Zig Ziglar

Encouraging others means helping people, looking for the best in them, and trying to bring out their positive qualities.

John Maxwell

Tip of the Day

When you're talking to somebody, ask yourself this question: "How can I be helpful?"

Prayer of the Day

Dear Lord, when I'm about to say
something, help me think about
my words before I say them, not after.
Amen

Honesty and Self-esteem

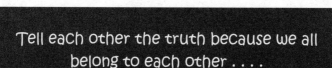

Tell each other the truth because we all
belong to each other . . . .

Ephesians 4:25 ICB

Have you ever said something that wasn't true? And after you said it, were you sorry that you told a lie? Well, if you were sorry, that's not surprising. When you don't tell the truth, you'll usually end up being sorry in the end.

Here's something that you're bound to learn sooner or later, you might as well learn it right now: Honesty and self-esteem go hand in hand. Why? Because it's hard to feel good about yourself if you're not being honest with other people.

So, if you want to feel better about yourself, do yourself a favor: tell the truth all the time. It's the right thing to do . . . and the best way to live!

Today, I am going to give you two tests:
one on trigonometry and one on honesty.
I hope you pass them both, but if you must
fail one, let it be trigonometry.

Madison Sarratt

The most exhausting thing in life
is being insincere.

Anne Morrow Lindbergh

Tip of the Day

Little white lies? Beware! You may think that
there's a big difference between "little" lies
and king-sized ones. Unfortunately, little
white lies have a tendency to grow into big
trouble . . . in a hurry.

Prayer of the Day

Dear Lord, I know that it's important
to be an honest person. Since I want
other people to be truthful with me,
let me be truthful with them,
today and every day.
Amen

God's Refrigerator

We know how much God loves us,
and we have put our trust in him.
God is love, and all who live in love live in
God, and God lives in them.

1 John 4:16 NLT

If God had a refrigerator in heaven, your picture would be on it! And that fact should make you feel very good about the person you are and the person you can become.

God's love for you is bigger and more wonderful than you can imagine, So do this, and do it right now: accept God's love with open arms and welcome His Son Jesus into your heart. When you do, you'll feel better about yourself . . . and your life will be changed forever.

God's love is unconditional, meaning
He always loves you, not just when
you do something right.

Seita Ann Jakes

Before anything else, above all else, beyond
everything else, God loves us. God loves us
extravagantly, ridiculously, without limit or
condition. God is in love with us . . .
God yearns for us.

Roberta Bondi

Tip of the Day

What a friend you have in Jesus: Jesus loves
you, and He offers you eternal life with Him
in heaven. Welcome Him into your heart.
Now!

Prayer of the Day

Dear God, the Bible teaches me that
Your love lasts forever. Thank You,
God, for Your love. Let me trust
Your promises, and let me live
according to Your teachings,
not just for today, but forever.
Amen

Selfishness Hurts.
Sharing Helps.

If you have two shirts, share with
the person who does not have one.
If you have food, share that too.

Luke 3:11 ICB

Learning how to share can be an important way to build better self-esteem. Why? Because when you learn to share your things, you'll know that you've done exactly what God wants you to do—and you'll feel better about yourself.

The Bible teaches that it's better to be generous than selfish. But sometimes, you won't feel like sharing your things, and you'll be tempted to keep everything for yourself. When you're feeling a little bit stingy, remember this: God wants you to share your things with people who need your help.

When you learn to be a more generous person, God will be pleased with you . . . and you'll be pleased with yourself.

Generosity is always wise.

Winston Churchill

I must admit that I personally measure success in terms of the contributions an individual makes to her or his fellow human beings.

Margaret Mead

Tip of the Day

What does the Bible say about sharing? It's simple: you should gladly share the things you have.

Prayer of the Day

Dear Lord, help me to learn
the importance of sharing. The Bible
teaches me to share, and so do my
parents. Now, it's up to me to learn
how to share the things that I have—
and it's up to me to share kind
words and good deeds
with my family and friends.
Amen

It's Great to Be You

You made my whole being; you formed me in my mother's body. I praise you because you made me in an amazing and wonderful way.

Psalm 139:13-14 NCV

How many people in the world are exactly like you? Only one—the person you see every time you look in the mirror. In other words, the only person in the world who's exactly like you . . . IS YOU! And that means you're special: special to God, special to your family, special to your friends, and a special addition to God's wonderful world!

But sometimes, when you are tired, angry, or sad, you may not feel very special. In fact, you may decide that you're not very special at all . . . but whenever you think like that, you're mistaken.

The Bible says that God made you in "an amazing and wonderful way." So the next time that you start feeling like you don't measure up, remember this: when God made all the people of the earth, He only made one you. And that means you're a V.I.P.

And what is a V.I.P.? A "Very Important Person," of course.

By the grace of God you are what you are;
glory in your selfhood, accept yourself
and go on from there.

Wilferd Peterson

It is no exaggeration to say that a strong
positive self-image is the best possible
preparation for success in life.

Joyce Brothers

Tip of the Day

Appearances, appearances, appearances . . .
Don't be too worried about what you look
like on the outside . . . be more concerned
about the kind of person you are on the
inside. God loves you just like you are . . . and
now, it's your turn to do the same thing.

Prayer of the Day

Dear Lord, I am a very lucky person, and I thank You for my blessings. Help me to be a good person, and help me use my talents and my possessions for Your Glory . . . and for Your Son. Amen

Your Best Friend

And I am convinced that nothing can ever separate us from his love. Whether we are high above the sky or in the deepest ocean, nothing in all creation will ever be able to separate us from the love of God that is revealed in Christ Jesus our Lord.

Romans 8:38–39 NLT

Do you know that Jesus loves you? And have you thought about exactly what His love should mean to you? Well, Christ's love should make you feel better about your life, your family, your future, and yourself.

There's an old song that says, "What a friend we have in Jesus." Those words are certainly true! When you invite Him into your heart, Jesus will be your friend forever.

Jesus wants you to have a happy, healthy life. He wants you to behave yourself, and He wants you to feel good about yourself. And now, it's up to you to do your best to live up to the hopes and dreams of your very best friend: Jesus.

The love of Christ is a fierce thing.
It can take the picture you have of yourself
and burn it in the fire of his loving eyes,
replacing it with a true masterpiece.

Sheila Walsh

He loved us not because we're lovable,
but because He is love.

C. S. Lewis

Tip of the Day

Jesus loves you . . . His love is amazing, it's
wonderful, and it's meant for you.

Prayer of the Day

Dear Lord, thank You for Your Son.
Jesus loves me and He shares so much
with me. Let me share His love with
others so that through me,
they can understand what it means
to follow Him.
Amen

Bible Verses
to Memorize

Thanks be to God
for his indescribable gift!

2 Corinthians 9:15 NIV

Unfailing love surrounds those who
trust the LORD.

Psalm 32:10 NLT

You are the light of the world.

Matthew 5:14 NIV

Above all, love each other deeply,
because love covers
a multitude of sins.

1 Peter 4:8 NIV

Do not neglect the spiritual gift
that is within you . . . .

1 Timothy 4:14 NASB

So let us try to do what makes peace
and helps one another.

Romans 14:19 NCV

He did it with all his heart,
and prospered.

2 Chronicles 31:21 KJV

All have sinned and are not
good enough for God's glory.

Romans 3:23 NCV

Love one another deeply, from the heart.

1 Peter 1:22 NIV

My purpose is to give life
in all its fullness.

John 10:10 HCSB

Be still, and know that I am God . . . .

Psalm 46:10 KJV

Those who are pure
in their thinking are happy,
because they will be with God.

Matthew 5:8 NCV

Grow in grace and understanding of
our Master and Savior,
Jesus Christ. Glory to the Master,
now and forever! Yes!

2 Peter 3:18 MSG

When I was a child,
I spoke and thought and reasoned
as a child does. But when I grew up,
I put away childish things.

1 Corinthians 13:11 NLT

Out of the abundance of the heart
the mouth speaks.

Matthew 12:34 NKJV

Love is patient;
love is kind.

1 Corinthians 13:4 HCSB

Your attitude should be the same that Christ Jesus had.

Philippians 2:5 NLT

God is our refuge and strength,
a very present help in trouble.

Psalm 46:1 KJV

Jesus said,
"Don't let your hearts be troubled.
Trust in God, and trust in me."

John 14:1 NCV